PRA

Margaret Pawl
British parents, a
in the course o
service with the s
History at Oxfor   much involved
in adult education in Britain and abroad – for
some years holding the position of tutor at the
Open University. Her books include a study
of Anglican-Roman Catholic relations, a bi-
ography of Donald Coggan, and two collections
of prayers, *Praying with the English Tradition*
and *Prayers for Pilgrims*.

Also by Margaret Pawley

Donald Coggan, Servant of Christ
Praying with the English Tradition
Prayers for Pilgrims

PRAYING
FOR PEOPLE

Compiled and edited by

MARGARET PAWLEY

Foreword by

Wendy Craig

First published 1992
Triangle
SPCK
Holy Trinity Church
Marylebone Road
London NW1 4DU

British Library Cataloguing in Publication Data
A catalogue record for this book is available
from the British Library.

ISBN 0-281-0458905

Typeset by Rowland Phototypesetting Ltd
Bury St Edmunds, Suffolk
Printed and bound in Great Britain by
BPCC Hazells Ltd
Member of BPCC Ltd

Contents

Foreword

Dear God, bless Mummy and Daddy, Grandma and Grandpa, and my guinea pig, and make my brother's sore thumb better and make me a good girl please. Amen.

Off would come slippers and dressing gown, and then I'd quickly snuggle down under the blankets, feeling cosy and dutiful and totally assured that these simple prayers would be answered.

In childhood we are happy to include people in our prayers. Huge lists are recited and we search our minds in case anyone we love may have been overlooked. True, our prayers are augmented with personal requirements; 'Please may I have a new record-player for Christmas', or 'Help me, God, to pass my exams this term'. Nothing wrong with that, but on the whole, the natural desire seems to be to put in a plea for those close to us or for people who need help. God engraves intercession on the human heart. Even non-believing adults cry out 'God, help them!' for those faced with catastrophe. Witness in this book pleas both passionate and gentle, from ancient times to the present day, asking Him to pour out His grace on others as well as ourselves. They come from the pens of poets and bishops, housewives and grannies, broadcasters and teachers, people from all walks of life who feel the need to pray for people.

When I first renewed my Faith eight years ago, I often felt guilty about the long list of petitions I submitted during my prayers. I questioned my motivation. I asked myself: am I praying for people because I think God will be pleased with me for being so selfless, in putting the considerations of others first? Or am I actually being selfish, inasmuch as life would be a great deal more comfortable for me if I didn't have to worry about the problems and pain of my loved ones, God having answered my prayers favourably? Then again I wondered, am I just doing what I've been taught, speaking for others, even when unlike our Lord, I may not even like them? Perhaps it was a mixture of all three, but I sensed that when I prayed, there was a genuine feeling of compassion and an unborn need to take the problems of others to the highest authority.

Even so, as an immature Christian I had niggling doubts about my incentive to petition for people; that was until I looked to Jesus, and found in the Gospels the help I needed. Jesus *wants* us to pray for others. He has set us a wonderful example during His life on earth by constantly interceding for his fellow men and women. Even when pinned to the cross He asked the Father to forgive His persecutors: 'Forgive them, Father,' He cried, 'for they do not know what they are doing' (Luke 23.34). We know that He spent many hours in supplication on behalf of his followers (John 17.9), and He told them that after His death He would continue to intercede for them with the Father as their great high priest. Andrew Murray explains this so well when he writes, 'In heaven Christ lives to pray. His whole conversation with His Father is prayer – an asking and receiving of the fullness of the Holy Spirit for His people. God delights in nothing so much as in prayer. Shall we not learn to believe that the highest blessings of heaven will be unfolded to us as we pray more?'

It is in the character of Jesus to pray for others. It is also richly in His character to forgive our enemies as we bring them before God (Matthew 5.44). This book offers two such prayers to help us frame our own petitions. One is by Thomas à Kempis (page 50) and the other by Sir Thomas More (page 49). The latter reads:

Almighty God,
have mercy on all that bear me evil will,
    and would me harm,
    and their faults and mine together,
    by such easy, tender, merciful means,
    and your infinite wisdom best can devise,
        vouchsafe to amend and redress,
and make us saved souls in heaven together
    where we may ever live and love together
        with you and your blessed saints,
O glorious Trinity,
    for the bitter passion of our sweet Saviour Christ.

Reading through, I find in this book prayers for our families, for those in sickness and adversity, for neighbours and friends, schools and colleges, for the ministry of the church, leaders of the country, the disabled, unemployed, homeless and many, many more. I'm sure that most human need is covered by this comprehensive selection of heartfelt appeals to God.

As an aid to intercession it is invaluable, for nothing unites us with others more than praying for them. How can we not grow to love them when we are asking God's blessing on them? We could not be so immovable. How can we feel alone and isolated when we are told in all certainty that Christ and the great heavenly host are praying with us? How can we feel at a loss for the right cause or words when we can call upon the Word of God and the Holy Spirit to help us? Psalm 37 tells us: 'Delight thyself in the Lord, and He shall give thee the desires of thine heart'. With this book to help us, let us gladly take all our petitions to Him in faith, and expect to receive.

I would like to share with you two prayers I love. The first by Andrew Murray is one I found myself which is now included in this book (page 41). It reads:

Dear Heavenly Father,
I am prone to pray for material blessing for others.
I am inclined to intercede for their health or for their
  jobs.
Worse, I am inclined to pray only for myself and my
  family!
Grant me that eternal perspective that shows concern
  for their salvation,
that shows concern for the spiritual blessings and
  values
that can give meaning and purpose to life.
Help me to be sensitive to the real needs of others,
and make me aware of the heavenly blessings you want
  them to have.
Guide me by your indwelling Spirit to pray right for
  them and not just for myself.
Amen.

The second (page 27) certainly speaks for grannies like
me:

A Grandmother's Prayer

> Lord,
> teach me to love my grandchildren
> as a grandmother should:
> not interfering,
> only understanding;
> not pushing myself,
> just being there when wanted.
> Teach me to be the sort of grandmother
> my children
> and my children's children
> would want me to be.
>
> Rosa George

Wendy Craig
November 1991

Introduction

We pray for those we love because we cannot help it. Especially in emergencies, it seems the most natural and effective way of reacting to a frightening situation which threatens someone near and dear, and often more importantly still, awakens our own perception of the significance of such a threat to us personally.

This is the sense in which many people pray – not just religious believers; so much so that it is often taken for granted that praying is just asking. This is clearly not so; there are types of prayer in which no specific petitions are made – such as in contemplative, meditative or listening prayers. The reason behind such prayer is to establish a relationship between men and women and the Creator God. When we have such a relationship, to include petitions for various people and causes close to the heart, within the ongoing prayer, seems entirely right. The Lord's Prayer, given by Jesus to his disciples, contains a good example of such a request within such a context.

> Give us this day our daily bread.
> Forgive us our sins
> as we forgive those who sin against us.

follows our recognition of the Creator as Father and acknowledges our dependence as creatures:

> Our Father in heaven,
> hallowed be your name.

These *asking* prayers – in support of people – in this book are designed both for men and women who have

xi

their own familiar patterns of prayer, and for those who, more recently or suddenly, have become aware of the need to pray for others, as a way of expressing longings for their well-being. In everyday life we might hesitate to ask favours of a stranger, but we know that God welcomes petitionary prayer, even when it is the only prayer that is offered. 'Ask', said Jesus in the Sermon on the Mount.

Praying has to start somewhere. Praying for others, or ourselves, can be an important starting point in a prayer life, because these are concerns very real to us. William Barclay, a prominent Scottish theologian,[1] has some wise advice at this point:

> Prayer is simply taking life to God . . . remembering that God is not only the rescuer when things get beyond us, but the friend with whom we live day by day. . . . If we keep prayer for the crisis, when the crisis comes we may find we cannot pray.

The value or effectiveness of petitionary prayer has recently been debated once again, and a variety of opinion has been aired. At one extent of the compass there has been talk of prayer for others as 'effort to change God's mind'; another gives a more cosmic interpretation that prayer increases the pool of spiritual energy in the world which can be devoted to the benefit of those who need. Attempts to explain the mystery of how prayer works in a material sense are usually unsatisfactory. Explanation must come by way of human experience and observation within a life of faith.

People throughout the world feel the need to pray. The Old and New Testaments are full of encouragement that men and women *should* pray to God for one another. In the Old Testament, this was a consequence upon the understanding that theirs was a personal God with whom a covenant had been made, and whose purposes would become clear. The prophet Jeremiah received the request 'Pray for us to the Lord your God'[2]; and Samuel likewise 'Pray for us your servants to the Lord your God, to save us from death'.[3] In the New Testament, a fresh covenant of love and peace was introduced with the incarnation of Jesus into the world and the concept of the Kingdom. His disciples were inspired not only to pray for this event – Thy Kingdom come – , but also for one another.

On the night before he died Jesus prayed for his disciples: 'those whom you have given me, because they belong to you'.[4] St Paul in his epistles provides countless examples of having prayed for the Christians of the young churches of Asia Minor. He wrote to the Colossians 'We have not stopped praying for you',[5] and to the group surrounding Timothy:

> I urge that requests, prayers, intercessions and thanksgivings be offered for everyone . . . such prayer is right and pleases God our Saviour whose will is that all men should find salvation and come to know the truth.[6]

So it was seen as right and good to pray for people. The writers of the prayers in this collection provide further evidence. Rescue was never assumed to be guaranteed to be immediate, though situations were desperate. Job asked bluntly 'Why should a man be born to wander blindly, hedged in by God on every side?'[7] And Jesus himself cried from the cross 'My God, my God why have you forsaken me?' The lesson that many have learnt from long-term praying is that there are not necessarily short-term answers. Yet the overwhelming evidence is that answers come. Jesus rose from the dead after three days and the descendants of Paul's first Christians now number millions and cover the globe.

Answers to prayer take into account God's purposes

for the whole, as well as the one; for the Kingdom, as well as for the single lost sheep; here is the meaning of 'your will be done'. To quote from William Barclay again: Prayer is not escape, either for ourselves or for others;

> Prayer is the way to conquest; the way of meeting the human situation . . . what we expect is that divine help in which everything becomes victory. . . . In prayer a human being is put in touch with a larger world and a larger life; in touch with that which is beyond.

Neville Ward[8] put it thus

> When any individual is in a right relationship with God, he contributes to making the whole universe, in which his friends also have their, maybe painful being, that much more 'right', fulfilled (as Christians have been taught to imagine plenitude), mobile, sensitive to the divine action. When only one person is in right relation to God, the whole universe, as it affects mankind, is nearer its divine intention, and that much . . . more receptive of the redemptive presence of God.

Both William Barclay and Neville Ward emphasise that prayer does not look like this to many people and also that praying involves personal involvement in the answer to the prayer: a willingness to be *used* in the granting of a petition.

It would seem that to pray for others means losing some part of ourselves, to offer it in love to a God who has revealed himself as love, for the benefit of someone else. Long experience down the ages has shown that strength and blessings can come both to the person who prays, as well as the person being prayed for. Crisis-praying can become less hectic and wordy, less of a monologue; requests can widen, increase, change until, in Evelyn Underhill's words, they include the whole world which needs this link with God's grace so much.

Words are not necessarily required to commend another human being to the goodness of God. It is often enough to hold them up by name in faith, hope and love. As T. S. Eliot wrote:

> And prayer is more
> Than an order of words, the conscious occupation
> Of the praying mind, or the sound of the voice
> praying.[9]

But for many, the words of Christians who spent their lives praying for others are helpful. In a letter to *The Times*, William Temple acknowledged with his characteristic skill with words, that it had been he who had been responsible for writing a prayer for the nation at a time of serious economic depression in 1931:

> There are some devout Christians who desire to be assisted in the concentration of their thoughts by specific reference to the immediate occasion.

It is in this spirit that this collection is offered.

The prayers in this book range from earliest times: the words of martyrs of early Christianity, those of Anselm written in about 1075, have such timeless modes of expression that they can represent the hopes of late-twentieth century Christians as adequately as prayers written today. Prayers come from all over the world: from the USA, from Africa, Italy, France, the Hebrides, as well as England; also from various Christian traditions. I have been unashamedly nostalgic in choosing to include the famous 'Eternal Father strong to save', in the hope that there will be others who, like me, will be transported back to their school days; to remember not only singing the hymn, but also reviving the vivid youthful image it created, of sailors in their lonely, dangerous lives. There are also some very simple prayers for use by young children, as well as longer prayers written in a more complex form as poetry. This variety will, I hope, mean that there is something here for everyone. It has not been easy to find specific prayers for all relationships; I should have liked to include grandparents, uncles and aunts, brothers and sisters, whose contributions are so rich in every life. Many petitionary prayers tend to be rather general, a tendency I have taken pains to avoid. It is difficult to identify with prayers for 'all sorts and conditions of men'.

Among writers of prayers there are giants whose works claim a place in any collection, and they are represented here: Lancelot Andrewes, Jeremy Taylor, Samuel Johnson, John Wesley and, in this century, George Appleton. Their petitionary prayers have qualities which make them immediately acceptable for use as our own: direct unsentimental language, no mere pious hopes nor wish for magic spells, but filled with realism that is visionary also.

A word on prayers that have been omitted. I regret being able to include only one prayer by Thomas Cranmer whose language and form are second to none in their beauty and intent. But they did not suit this selection; few of his petitionary prayers were for individuals. Neither have I included angry prayers, though I do not doubt that prayer, to be authentic, can include anger; it is certainly part of bereavement. Thus Dylan Thomas's powerful:

Do not go gentle into that good night . . .
Rage, rage against the dying of the light.[10]

on the death of his father, does not have a place here. The anger has to be our own. And so, of course, must the prayers be. The words placed in this book are merely landmarks.

Margaret Pawley
Wye, Kent,
1992

1 1907–78. Professor of Divinity and Biblical Criticism at Glasgow University.
2 Jeremiah 37.3
3 1 Samuel 12.19.
4 John 17.9.
5 Colossians 1.9.
6 1 Timothy 2.1–4.
7 Job 3.23.
8 Neville Ward is a Methodist minister and writer of books on prayer; this is taken from his *The Use of Praying* (Epworth Press 1967).
9 *Little Gidding* I, lines 45–47 from *Four Quartets* in *Collected Poems 1909–1962* (Faber 1963).
10 'Do not go gentle . . . ' from *Collected Poems* (Dent 1954).

PRAYERS
FOR FAMILIES

For a child at birth

O God our Father,
    we give you thanks
    for this little child
    who has come to us from you.

Bless him/her now
    and through all the days
    of his/her life.

Protect him in the days of his helplessness;
    bring him in safety
    through childhood's dangers;
    and grant that he may grow to manhood,
    and do a good day's work
    and witness for you.

Help us his parents so to love him
    and so to train him
    that we shall not fail
    in the trust which you have
    given to us, and that,
    even as you have given him to us,
    we may give him back in dedication to you:
    through Jesus Christ our Lord.

WILLIAM BARCLAY 1907–78, *Presbyterian minister, scholar, preacher and broadcaster. He worked on the translation of the New English Bible and won popular acclaim for his Bible study notes and books of prayers.*

For an infant

Dear Babe, that sleepest cradled by my side,
Whose gentle breathings, heard in this deep calm,
Fill up the interspersèd vacancies
And momentary pauses of the thought!
My babe so beautiful! it thrills my heart
With tender gladness, thus to look at thee,
And think that thou shalt learn far other lore,
And in far other scenes! For I was reared
In the great city, pent 'mid cloisters dim,
And saw nought lovely but the sky and stars.
But *thou*, my babe! shalt wander like a breeze
By lakes and sandy shores, beneath the crags
Of ancient mountain, and beneath the clouds,
Which image in their bulk both lakes and shores
And mountain crags: so shalt thou see and hear
The lovely shapes and sounds intelligible
Of that eternal language, which thy God
Utters, who from eternity doth teach
Himself in all, and all things in himself.
Great universal Teacher! he shall mould
Thy spirit, and by giving make it ask.

Therefore all seasons shall be sweet to thee,
Whether the summer clothe the general earth
With greenness, or the redbreast sit and sing
Betwixt the tufts of snow on the bare branch
Of mossy apple-tree, while the nigh thatch
Smokes in the sun-thaw; whether the eave-drops fall
Heard only in the trances of the blast,
Or if the secret ministry of frost
Shall hang them up in silent icicles,
Quietly shining to the quiet moon.

SAMUEL TAYLOR COLERIDGE 1772–1834, *an English
poet who advocated a more spiritual and religious
interpretation of life than some of his contemporaries. This
extract comes from a poem called 'Frost at midnight'.*

4

For an infant

'I have no name
I am but two days old.'
What shall I call thee?
'I happy am,
Joy is my name.'
Sweet joy befall thee!

Pretty joy,
Sweet joy, but two days old.
Sweet joy I call thee.
Thou doth smile,
I sing the while.
Sweet joy befall thee.

WILLIAM BLAKE *1757–1827, a mystical poet of
considerable imagination who wrote several poems on the
theme of young children. This poem is entitled 'Infant Joy'.*

For the newly-baptised

Richard, run ryghte
In Life's race:
Christ thy myghte,
His thy grace;
His thy lyghte
Round thy wayes
All thy dayes.

Prayer for Richard Southby, grandson of Lady Southby; transcribed by B. C. Boulter.

For a newly-baptised child

Yours be the blessing of God and the Lord,
The perfect Spirit his blessing afford,
The Trinity's blessing on you outpoured
With gentle and gen'rous shedding abroad,
So gently gen'rously for you unstored.

Traditional Gaelic prayer.

For children – in thanksgiving

I send my heart to thee in thanks for these little
ones: for the strange uprising of happiness that
comes to me as my eye follows them.

Sweet is the music of their wind-borne laughter,
yea, sweeter than all musics.

I listen to them, and am one with the mavis and
the dawn and the flower.

And then I wonder what thy thought is of them –
thy children. Yet I need not wonder. For I look
upward and lo! thou art leaning out over the
window of heaven, and thou art smiling.

Prayer by an eighty year-old man.

For children

Thou seest me, Father, stand before my cottage
door, watching my little ones at play.

O thou, to whom to love and to be are one, hear my
faith-cry for them who are more thine than mine.

Give each of them what is best for each. I cannot
tell what it is. But thou knowest. I only ask thou
love them and keep them with the loving and
keeping thou dost show to Mary's son and thine.

*Prayer by a Hebridean mother. From a collection of prayers
in the Celtic tradition.*

9

For children

Bless my children with healthful bodies,
with good understandings,
with the graces and gifts of thy Spirit,
with sweet dispositions
and holy habits,
and sanctify them throughout
in their bodies, souls and spirits,
and keep them unblameable
to the coming of our Lord Jesus.

JEREMY TAYLOR *1613–67, bishop successively of various
Irish sees; a scholar and writer of devotional works,
including many prayers.*

For children

O God of love and mercy,
help us to understand our children
as they grow in years
and in knowledge of your world.
Make us compassionate for their temptations and
    failures
and encouraging in their seeking
after truth and value
for their lives.
Stir in us
appreciation of their ideals
and sympathy for their frustrations;
that with them
we may look for a better world
than either we or they have known,
through Jesus Christ,
our common Lord and Master. Amen.

MASSEY HAMILTON SHEPHERD, Jnr b. 1913, priest of
the Episcopal Church of the USA.

For children

God of love, we pray for our children
as they grow up in our family circle.
Give us understanding of their needs,
and show us how best we can help them
as they face their problems
and prepare for the life of the world.
Help us to establish a relationship of trust
between them and ourselves,
and to make our home a place where
at all times they may find love and security;
in Christ's name.

FRANK COLQUHOUN *b. 1909, a Canon Residentiary of*
Southwark and later Vice-Dean of Norwich; he is a writer
and collector of prayers.

For children

O heavenly Father,
bless our children
  whom you have given us.
May they grow up to be wise,
          loving,
          generous,
          holy and
          unselfish;
may their lives be dedicated to thee
  in whatever way is in accordance
          with thy will,
and may they continue to be a blessing
  to us and to others. Amen.

IAN WHITE-THOMSON *b. 1904, Dean of Canterbury
1963–76. He and his wife said this prayer each evening for
their four children for many years.*

'Prayer for my daughter'

Once more the storm is howling, and half hid
Under this cradle-hood and coverlid
My child sleeps on. There is no obstacle
But Gregory's wood and one bare hill
Whereby the haystack- and roof-levelling wind,
Bred on the Atlantic, can be stayed;
And for an hour I have walked and prayed
Because of the great gloom that is in my mind.

I have walked and prayed for this young child an
    hour
And heard the sea-wind scream upon the tower,
And under the arches of the bridge, and scream
In the elms above the flooded stream;
Imagining in excited reverie
That the future years had come,
Dancing to a frenzied drum,
Out of the murderous innocence of the sea.

May she be granted beauty and yet not
Beauty to make a stranger's eye distraught,
Or hers before a looking-glass, for such,
Being made beautiful overmuch,
Consider beauty a sufficient end,
Loss natural kindness and maybe
The heart-revealing intimacy
That chooses right, and never find a friend . . .

In courtesy I'd have her chiefly learned;
Hearts are not had as a gift but hearts are earned
By those that are not entirely beautiful;
Yet many, that have played the fool
For beauty's very self, has charm made wise,
And many a poor man that has roved,
Loved and thought himself beloved,
From a glad kindness cannot take his eyes.

May she become a flourishing hidden tree
That all her thoughts may like the linnet be,
And have no business but dispensing round
Their magnanimities of sound,
Nor but in merriment begin a chase,
Nor but in merriment a quarrel.
O may she live like some green laurel
Rooted in one dear perpetual place.

And may her bridegroom bring her to a house
Where all's accustomed, ceremonious;
For arrogance and hatred are the wares
Peddled in the thoroughfares.
How but in custom and in ceremony
Are innocence and beauty born?
Ceremony's a name for the rich horn,
And custom for the spreading laurel tree.

W. B. YEATS 1865–1939, *Irish poet who wrote this prayer between February and June 1919.*

For a son – in bereavement

Farewell, thou child of my right hand and joy;
  My sin was too much hope of thee, lov'd boy,
Seven years thou wert lent to me, and I thee pay,
  Exacted by my fate, on the just day.
O, could I loose all father now. For why
  Will man lament the state he should envie?
To have so soone scap'd worlds, and fleshes rage,
  And, if no other miserie, yet age?
Rest in soft peace, and, ask'd say here doth lye
  Ben Jonson his best piece of poetrie.
For whose sake, hence-forth, all his vowes be such,
  As what he loves may never like too much.

BEN JONSON 1572–1637, *English poet, playwright and actor.*

Children's prayers for their parents

Lord Jesus Christ,
I praise and thank you for my parents
and my brothers and sisters,
whom you have given me to cherish.
Surround them with your tender, loving care,
teach them to love and serve one another
in true affection,
and to look to you in all their needs.
I place them all in your care,
knowing that your love for them
is greater than my own.
Keep us close to one another in this life
and conduct us at the last
to our true heavenly home.
Blessed be God for ever. Amen.

MICHAEL BUCKLEY *b. 1924, a Monsignor involved in the
ministry of healing who has compiled several widely-used
books of prayers, including* The Treasury of the Holy Spirit.

Prayers for children to use

Holy God,
    Creator and Father,
    thank you for our family,
    thank you for your loving care of all of us,
    all through the day,
    in everything and everywhere,
    and while we sleep.

Help me to remember that you are
always with me, Lord.
Help me to remember you in the good times,
Not just to call for help when things go wrong.

Thank you, God, for everything you
have made in your world, and
bless all who live in it
especially –
For all the wrong things I have said
and done, forgive me, Lord.
And help me to be able to say sorry
to those I hurt.

Thank you, God, for being with me always.

The Mothers' Union.

We thank you,
God our Father,
for your love in giving so much to us.
Help us to remember
that your gifts are meant for everyone.
Help us to find ways of sharing
with those who are poor or hungry.
For your love's sake. Amen.

JOHN D. SEARLE

Heavenly Father,
look in love on all our friends and neighbours.
Keep them from harm,
deepen our friendship with them
and may we grow in love of you,
our Saviour and friend. Amen.

MICHAEL BOTTING *b. 1925, incumbent in Cheshire;
Honorary Canon of Ripon Cathedral since 1982.*

Young children's prayers

In the morning

Thank you, Lord Jesus, for protecting me during the
    night.
Now in this new day, help me to be kind to
    everyone.
Bless my family and all I love. Amen.

In the evening

Thank you, Lord Jesus, for my happy day.
Forgive any unkind things I have done.
Watch over us all as we sleep, and bless my family
    and all my friends.

ENID BLYTON *1897–1968, a prolific writer of children's
books.*

For parents

Lord,
Keep my parents in your love.
Lord,
bless them and keep them.
Lord,
please let me have money and strength
and keep my parents for many more years
so that I can take care of them.

Prayer of a young Ghanian Christian.

For parents – a son's or a daughter's prayer

Thank you, if the passing of the years has made me understand my parents better, and has made me love them more, and has drawn me closer and closer to them.

Forgive me, if I have taken everything for granted, if sometimes I just made use of my home, if I took everything and gave nothing.

Forgive me, if sometimes I have been difficult to live with, irritable, rebellious, disobedient, uncommunicative, impatient of advice, angry at restraint.

Help me at least to try to do something to show my gratitude, and to try to repay the debt I owe, even if it never can be fully repaid.

Help me so to value my home, so to love my parents, so to show them that I love them, that some day, when they are gone and I look back, I may have nothing to regret.

Hear this my prayer for Jesus' sake. Amen.

WILLIAM BARCLAY *See note on p. 3.*

For a child going to school for the first time

O God our Father,
   as our child goes to school for the first time,
   we are anxious at this first step away from home.
Keep him/her safe
   from all that would hurt him/her in body
   or harm him/her in mind.

Help him to be happy at school
   and to know the joy of learning
   and of making friendships
   with other boys and girls.

Help him to learn well
   that he may grow up
   to stand on his own feet,
   to earn his own living,
   and to serve you and his fellow-men;

through Jesus Christ our Lord.

WILLIAM BARCLAY. *See note on p. 3.*

For members of a family on a marriage

O God, our Father,
   whose greatest gift is love,
bless those, we ask you,
   who today within your presence
will take each other in marriage.

We thank you that they have
   found such love and faith
   and trust in each other
that they wish to take each other
   to have and to hold
   all the days of their life.
Let nothing ever come between them,
   but throughout all the chances
   and changes of life,
   keep them for ever loving
   and for ever true.

Keep them safe from illness,
   from poverty,
   and from all the trouble
   which would hurt them in any way.
But if any trial does come to them,
   grant that it may only drive them
   closer together, and closer to you.

Grant to them through all their days
   the perfect love which many waters
   cannot quench and which is stronger
   than death itself;

through Jesus Christ our Lord.

WILLIAM BARCLAY. *See note on p. 3.*

For families

Heavenly Father,
from whom all parenthood comes,
teach us so to understand our children
that they may grow in your wisdom and love
according to your holy will.

Fill us with sensitive respect
for the great gift of human life
which you have committed
to our care,
help us to listen with patience
to their worries and problems
and give us the tolerance
to allow them to develop
as individuals.

For your name's sake.

MICHAEL BUCKLEY. *See note on p. 17.*

For families

Most gracious Father,
this is our home;
let your peace rest upon it.
Let love abide here,
love of one another,
love of mankind,
love of life itself,
and love of God.
Let us remember that
as many hands build a house,
so many hearts make a home.

HUGH BLACKBURNE *b. 1912, Suffragan Bishop of Thetford 1977–80.*

A grandmother's prayer

Lord,
teach me to love my grandchildren
as a grandmother should:
not interfering,
only understanding;
not pushing myself,
just being there when wanted.
Teach me to be the sort of grandmother
my children
and my children's children
would want me to be

ROSA GEORGE

For husband and wife

Heavenly Father,
Marriage is of your making.
It is you who have joined us together
   as man and wife.
We pray that throughout our married life
   you will give us grace at all times
      to be true to one another,
      to consider one another's needs,
      to support one another in trouble,
      to forgive one another's mistakes,
      to love one another to the end.
So may we as man and wife enjoy your constant
   blessing and live together for your glory.

FRANK COLQUHOUN. *See note on p. 12.*

A father's prayer for his wife and family

O God, help me to be true to the great privilege and the great responsibility which you have given to me.

Help me to be an example and a friend to my children, and a real partner to my wife.

Don't let me get so busy with work and with outside things that I am almost a stranger in my own home, and that I take no interest in household things.

Don't let me take all that is done for me for granted, and help me to keep love alive within the home.

Keep me from habits which make the work of the house harder, and from ways which irritate and annoy, or which get on the nerves of those who live with me.

Give me health and strength and work to do, to earn a living for those who depend on me and whom I love so much; but help me to remember that love is always more important than money.

O God, you have given me the name of father; you have given me your own name; help me to be true to it.

This I ask for your love's sake. Amen.

WILLIAM BARCLAY. *See note on p. 3.*

A mother's prayer for her husband and family

O God, help me always to remember that you have given to me the most important task in the world, the task of making a home.

Help me to remember this when I am tired of making beds, and washing clothes, and cooking meals, and cleaning floors, and mending clothes, and standing in shops. Help me to remember it when I am physically tired in body, and when I am weary in mind with the same things which have to be done again and again, day in and day out.

Help me never to be irritable, never to be impatient, never to be cross. Keep me always sweet. Help me to remember how much my husband and my children need me, and help me not to get annoyed when they take me for granted, and when they never seem to think of the extra work they sometimes cause me.

Help me to make this home such that the family will always be eager to come back to it, and such that, when the children grow up and go out to their own homes, they will have nothing but happy memories of the home from which they have come.

This I ask for your love's sake. Amen.

WILLIAM BARCLAY. *See note on p. 3.*

Prayer of a wife for her husband

O most glorious God,
and my most indulgent Lord and gracious Father,
    who dost bless us by thy bounty,
    pardon us by thy grace,
    and govern by thy providence,
bless and preserve that dear person
    whom thou hast chosen to be my husband;
let his life be long and blessed,
    comfortable and holy;
and let me also be a great blessing
    and comfort to him,
    a sharer in all his joys,
    a refreshment in all his sorrows,
    a meet helper for him
    in all accidents and chances of the world.
Make me amiable for ever in his eyes,
    and very dear to him.
Unite his heart to me in the dearest union
    of love and holiness;
and mine to him in all sweetness,
    charity and compliance . . .
that we may delight in each other
    according to thy blessed word
    and ordinance,
and both of us may rejoice in thee,
    having our portion in the love
    and service of God for ever and ever.

JEREMY TAYLOR. *See note on p. 10.*

31

To a wife

I look up, you pass
I have to reconcile your
existence and the meaning of it
with what I read: kings and queens
and their battles
for power. You have your battle,
too. I ask myself: Have
I been on your side? Lovelier
dead queen than a live
wife? History worships
the fact but cannot remain
neutral. Because there are no kings
worthy of you; because poets
better than I are not here
to describe you; because time
is always too short, you must go by
now without mention, as unknown
to the future as to
the past, with one man's
eyes resting on you
in the interval of his concern.

R. S. THOMAS b. 1913, poet and priest of the church in
Wales; this poem is entitled 'Marriage'.

32

For a future wife

Most glorious Lord of Lyfe that on this day,
Didst make thy triumph over death and sin;
and having harrowed hell didst bring away
captivity then captive us to win;
this joyous day, deare Lord, with joy begin,
and grant that we for whom thou diddest dye
being with thy deare blood clene washt from sin,
may live for ever in felicity.
And that thy love we weighing worthily,
may likewise love thee for the same againe;
and for thy sake that all lyke deare didst buy,
with love may one another entertaine.
  So let us love, deare love, lyke as we ought,
  love is the lesson which the Lord us taught.

EDMUND SPENSER *1552?–99, English poet; he wrote this
prayer on Easter Day with his future wife in mind. It is
Sonnet LXVIII in his collection entitled* Amoretti.

33

For husbands and wives

Eternal God, author of harmony and happiness, we
thank you for the gift of marriage in which men and
women seek and find fulfilment, companionship, and
the blessing of family life.
>Give patience to those who look forward to
>marriage.
>Give courage to those who face trials within their
>marriage.
>Give comfort to those whose marriage has
>broken.
>Give gratitude to those whose marriages are
>successful and fruitful, and let their lives reflect
>your love and glory.

Through Jesus Christ our Lord.

MICHAEL SAWARD *b. 1932, Canon of St Paul's
Cathedral, formerly Vicar of Ealing, and a popular
hymnwriter.*

O God, our heavenly Father,
we pray for your grace and blessing for . . .
as they make their marriage vows.
Let their love for each other be deep and lasting;
give them understanding of each other's mind and
needs;
help them to share their joys and sorrows
and keep faithful to their promises to live together
until death,
through Jesus Christ who
blessed the wedding at Cana by his presence.

Mothers' Union prayer.

Of a wife – in bereavement

So close the ground, and 'bout her shade
Black curtains draw: my bride is laid.
Sleep on, my love, in thy cold bed
Never to be disquieted.
My last good night! Thou wilt not wake
Till I thy fate shall overtake:
Till age, our grief, or sickness must
Marry my body to that dust
It so much loves; and fill the room
My heart keeps empty in thy tomb.
Stay for me there: I will not fail
To meet thee in that hollow vale.
And think not much of my delay;
I am already on the way,
And follow thee with all the speed
Desire can make, or sorrows breed.
Each minute is a short degree
And every hour a step towards thee.
At night when I betake to rest,
Next morn I rise nearer my west
Of life, almost by eight hours sail
Than when sleep breathed his drowsy gale . . .
But hark! my pulse, like a soft drum,
Beats my approach, tells thee I come;
And slow howe'er my marches be
I shall at last sit down by thee.
    The thought of this bids me go on
And wait my dissolution
With hope and comfort, Dear, (forgive
The crime) I am content to live
Divided, with but half a heart,
Till we shall meet and never part.

HENRY KING 1592–1669, *Bishop of Chichester, friend of
John Donne, Izaak Walton, and Ben Jonson, the poet. This
extract comes from a poem written on the death of his wife.*

For *absent members of families*

Heavenly Father, you are present everywhere
and care for all your children;
we commend to you the members of our families
who are now parted from us.
Watch over them and protect them from all harm;
surround them and us with your love;
and bring us all at last to that home
where partings are no more;
through Jesus Christ our Lord.

F. W. STREET

For in-laws

O God, our Father, we ask you to bless
those who have entered our family life through
    marriage.
We pray that our different backgrounds may bring
enrichment and a deeper understanding.
Take away mistrust, suspicion and possessiveness
and guide us by your spirit into a new bond
of love and affection,
through Christ our Lord.

Mothers' Union prayer.

PRAYERS
FOR FRIENDS

Praying for others

Dear Heavenly Father,
I am prone to pray for material blessings for others.
I am inclined to intercede for their health or for their jobs.
Worse, I am inclined to pray only for myself and my family!
Grant me that eternal perspective that shows concern for their salvation,
that shows concern for the spiritual blessings and values
that can give meaning and purpose to life.
Help me to be sensitive to the real needs of others,
and make me aware of the heavenly blessings you want them to have.
Guide me by your indwelling Spirit to pray right for them and not just for myself.
Amen.

ANDREW MURRAY 1828–1917, *minister in the Dutch Reformed Church and evangelistic preacher whose emphasis on prayer and personal holiness was expounded in numerous books, including* With Christ in the School of Prayer. *He took a keen interest in the welfare of the Africans to whom he ministered in South Africa.*

For friends

May the God of love
who is the source of all our affection
for each other formed here on earth
take our friendships into his keeping,
that they may continue and increase
throughout life and beyond it,
in Jesus Christ our Lord.

WILLIAM TEMPLE 1881–1944, *successively Bishop of Manchester, Archbishop of York and Archbishop of Canterbury. He was prominent in national and international fields in the interests of social and economic justice and Christian unity.*

For friends

Be pleased, O Lord, to remember my friends,
    all that have prayed for me,
    and all that have done me good.
Do thou good to them
    and return all their kindness
    double into their own bosom,
    rewarding them with blessings
    and sanctifying them with thy graces,
    and bringing them to glory . . .
Let all my family and kindred,
    my neighbours and acquaintances
    receive the benefit of my prayers,
    and the blessings of God;
the comforts and supports of thy providence,
    and the sanctification of thy spirit.

JEREMY TAYLOR. *See note on p. 10.*

For friends

Lord Jesus, thank you for being our friend,
and for enriching our lives
with so many gifts of your love.
Thank you for human friends
and for all they mean to us.
Thank you especially for those
who have helped us
and stood by us in difficult times.
Help us, who have received so much,
to give true friendship to others,
in your name
and for your sake.

FRANK COLQUHOUN. *See note on p. 12.*

For friends

I give thanks to my God for all my memories of you,
happy at all times in all the prayer I offer for all of
     you;
so full a part have you taken in the work of Christ's
     gospel,
from the day when it first reached you till now.
Nor am I less confident that
he who has inspired this generosity in you
will bring it to perfection,
ready for the day when Jesus Christ comes.
    It is only fitting that I should entertain such hopes
     for you;
you are close to my heart,
and I know that you all share my happiness
in being a prisoner, and being able to defend and
     assert
the truth of the gospel.
God knows how I long for you all,
with the tenderness of Jesus Christ himself.
    And this is my prayer for you;
may your love grow richer and richer yet,
in the fulness of its knowledge and the depth of its
     perception,
so that you may learn to prize what is of value;
may nothing cloud your consciences
or hinder your progress
till the day when Christ comes;
may you reap, through Jesus Christ,
the full harvest of your justification to God's glory
     and praise.

ST PAUL *died c AD 65. This extract comes from St Paul's
letter to the Christian community at Philippi in Macedonia;
this was the first of the churches he founded in Europe, so
they were close to him in affection (see Philippians 1. 3–11).*

For friends

Let us pray for our friends,
that they may lead happy and useful lives;
Let us pray for any friends
with whom we have quarrelled,
that we may have the chance to be reconciled;
Let us pray for those who are living in new
      surroundings
and lack friends.
Let us pray for those who have lost their friends
by the way they live;
Let us pray for those who befriend the friendless.
God our Father,
make us true and loyal friends.
Grant that all our friends
may lead us nearer you.

CARYL MICKLEM *b. 1925, a retired URC minister, hymn
writer and religious broadcaster.*

46

For friends far away

O heavenly Father,
who has bestowed on us
the comfort of earthly friends:
look in love upon those dear to us
from whom we are separated.
Protect them and keep them from harm;
prosper and bless them in all good things;
suffer them never to be desolate or afraid,
and let no shadow come between them and us
    to divide our hearts;
but in your own good time
may we renew the comfort of sight and sound;
    through Jesus Christ our Lord.

From the BBC's New Every Morning: *A book of daily prayers for broadcasting.*

For friends – for reconciliation

O Lord,
Give me strength to refrain
    from the unkind silence that is born
    of hardness of heart;
the unkind silence that clouds
    the serenity of understanding
    and is the enemy of peace.

Give me strength to be the first
    to tender the healing word
    and the renewal of friendship,
that the bonds of amity
    and the flow of charity
may be strengthened for the good of the brethren
    and the furthering
    of thine eternal, loving purpose.

CECIL HUNT

For our enemies – for reconciliation

Almighty God,
have mercy on all that bear me evil will,
    and would me harm,
  and their faults and mine together,
  by such easy, tender, merciful means,
  and your infinite wisdom best can devise,
    vouchsafe to amend and redress,
and make us saved souls in heaven together
  where we may ever live and love together
    with you and your blessed saints,
O glorious Trinity,
  for the bitter passion of our sweet Saviour Christ.

SIR THOMAS MORE *1478–1535, Lord Chancellor of England in 1529. In 1535 he was executed on the grounds of high treason for the opposition to the Act of Supremacy of Henry VIII.*

For those we have wronged

I offer up to you
my prayers and intercessions,
for those especially
who have in any matter hurt,
  grieved, or found fault with me,
  or who have done me
  any damage or displeasure.
For all those also whom, at any time,
  I have vexed,
  troubled,
  burdened,
  and scandalised,
  by words or deed,
  knowingly or in ignorance;
that you would grant us all equally
  pardon for our sins,
  and for our offences against
  each other.
Take away from our hearts, O Lord,
  all suspiciousness,
  indignation,
  wrath and contention,
  and whatsoever may hurt charity,
  and lessen brotherly love.

THOMAS Á KEMPIS *c.1380–1471, an Augustinian canon
of Zwolle in the Netherlands; author of* The Imitation of
Christ *from which this extract is taken.*

For friends

Jesus Christ, my dear and gracious Lord,
you have shown a love greater than that of any
    man . . .
Lord, who showed such love to your enemies,
you have also enjoined the same love upon your
    friends.

  My good Lord,
as your servant I long to pray to you for my friends,
but as your debtor I am held back by my sins.
    For I am not able to pray for my own pardon,
    how then can I dare to ask openly
    for your grace for others?
I anxiously seek intercessors on my own behalf,
how then shall I be so bold as to intercede for
    others?
What shall I do, Lord God, what shall I do?
You command me to pray for them
    and my love prompts me to do so,
    but my conscience cries out against me,
saying that I should be concerned about my own
    sins,
    so that I tremble to speak for others.

So I pray you, good and gracious God,
for those who love me for your sake
    and whom I love in you.
And I pray more earnestly for those
whom you know love me
    and whom I do most truly love.
I am not doing this, Lord,
    as being righteous and free from sin,
but as one urged on by some kind of love for others.

So love them, you source of love,
  by whose command and gift I love them;
and if my prayer does not deserve to avail for them
  because it is offered you by a sinner,
let it avail for them because it is made at your
  command.
  Love them, Author and Giver of love,
for your own sake, not for mine,
  and make them love you with all their heart,
all their soul, and all their mind,
so that they will speak and do
only what pleases you and is expedient for them.

Do this for them and with them, Lord,
so that they may speed according to your will,
and thus ruled and protected by you,
  always and everywhere,
may they come at last to glory and eternal rest,
  through you who are living and reigning God,
  through all ages. Amen.

ANSELM 1033–1109, *a native of Aosta who travelled to the Abbey of Bec in Normandy and became its Abbot; he later became one of the greatest Archbishops of Canterbury. Translated from Latin by Sister Benedicta Ward SLG.*

For enemies

Almighty and tender Lord Jesus Christ,
  I have asked you to be good to my friends,
and now I bring before you what I desire in my
  heart
      for my enemies.

You alone, Lord, are mighty;
  you alone are merciful;
  whatever you make me desire for my enemies,
  give it to them and give the same back to me,
      and if what I ask for them at any time
      is outside the rule of charity,
  whether through weakness, ignorance, or malice,
      good Lord, do not give it to them
      and do not give it back to me.
You who are the true light, lighten their darkness;
  you who are the whole truth, correct their errors;
  you who are the true life, give life to their souls.
For you have said to your beloved disciple
      that he who loves not remains dead.
So I pray, Lord, that you will give them love for
  you
      and love for their neighbour,
as far as you ordain that they should have it,
lest they should sin before you against their
  brother.

Your slave begs you for his fellow slaves,
      lest because of me they offend
against the kindness of so good and great a lord.
Let them be reconciled to you and in concord with
  me,
according to your will and for your own sake.

This is the punishment
that in the secret of my heart
I want to exact
for those who serve with me and those who sin with
me –
this is the punishment that I ask
for those who serve with me and hate me –
let us love you and each other
as you will and as is expedient for us,
so that we may make amends to the good Lord
for our own and for each other's offences;
so that we may obey with one heart in love
one Lord and one Master.
This is the revenge your sinner asks
on all who wish him evil and act against him.
Most merciful Lord,
prepare the same punishment for your sinner.

Fulfil my prayer, Lord, not only for my friends
and the enemies for whom I have prayed,
but distribute the healing of your mercy
wherever you know it may help anyone
and not be contrary to your will,
both to the living and the departed.
Hear me always with your favour,
not according as my heart wills or as my mouth
asks,
but as you know and will that I ought to wish and
ask,
O Saviour of the world,
who with the Father and the Holy Spirit
lives and reigns God
throughout all ages. Amen.

ANSELM. *See note on p. 52.*

For a friend in sickness

Cast him not away in the time of his weakness;
forsake him not now,
when his strength failest him.
In the multitude of the sorrows
that are in his heart,
let thy comforts, O Lord,
refresh his soul.
O Lord, when he is oppressed,
comfort thou him.
O Lord, let thy strength
be made perfect in his weakness.
Let not temptation oppress him,
but such as is common to thy children;
but as thou art faithful, O Lord,
so suffer him not to be tempted
above what he is able.
But good Lord, with the temptation give a happy
        issue,
that he may be able to overcome it.
O Lord, though he be afflicted on every side,
yet let him not be distressed;
though in want of some of thy comforts,
yet not of all;
though chastened, yet not forsaken;
though cast down, yet not destroyed.

LANCELOT ANDREWES *1555–1626, successively Bishop
of Chichester, Ely and Winchester. This prayer comes from* A
Manual for the Sick.

For the healing of a friend

May God, my dear, be thy healing one;

    I set my hand upon thee this day
    In name of Father,
    In name of Son,
    In name of Spirit of power, I pray,
       Three Persons who compass thee alway.

Traditional Gaelic prayer from IAN MACKAY, *crofter from Kinlochewe.*

PRAYERS FOR PEOPLE IN THE COMMUNITY

For those who serve us

Our Father,
we remember before you
those who serve us
in the everyday ministries of life:
doctors, dentists, nurses, teachers,
assistants in shops, banks and offices;
builders, plumbers, mechanics;
milkmen, postmen, dustmen.
Keep us mindful, O Lord,
of what they and others do for us,
and may we accept their services
with gratitude in Christ's name.

FRANK COLQUHOUN. *See note on p. 12.*

For those whose work is dangerous

Eternal Father, strong to save, we pray for those whose work is often dangerous and on whom the lives of others so largely depend:

> for members of the armed forces, the police and the fire brigades;
>
> for coastguards and those who man the lifeboats;
>
> for the crews of helicopters engaged in rescue service.

Uphold them, O God, in the fulfilment of their duties, and protect them in every peril of land and sea and air; we ask it in the name of Christ our Lord.

FRANK COLQUHOUN. *See note on p. 12.*

For farmers

We remember with gratitude, Father,
    the work of farmers in all parts of the world who
    provide our daily food.
May they all receive a fair return
    for their labour.
May their methods treat both
    animals and soil with care.
May they be spared the effects
    of disease and bad weather.

CARYL MICKLEM. *See note on p. 47.*

For members of the mass media

Father, we thank you that you have spoken to us
through the words of scripture,
and chiefly through him who is the living word of
   God.
   We pray for all who,
by what they say and write,
influence the lives of others;
for those whose daily task is in the use of words.
   We ask for them reverence for the truth,
sensitiveness to human need,
and a true concern for the welfare of the
   community;
through Jesus Christ our Lord.

BASIL NAYLOR *b. 1911, Canon Residentiary and
Chancellor of Liverpool Cathedral 1956–82.*

Lord God, you have placed in human hands
great power for good or evil through television.
   We pray for those whose faces and voices are thus
   known in millions of homes;
for those who decide policies and plan schedules;
and those who direct and produce programmes.
   We pray that their skills and gifts
may be devoted to what is true and good,
so that those who watch and listen
may be informed and entertained without being
   debased or corrupted;
through Jesus Christ our Lord.

CHRISTOPHER IDLE *b. 1938 hymnwriter and formerly
vicar of Limehouse in the East End of London.*

For seafarers

We pray for those who go to sea
    in ships large and small.
Defend them in bad weather;
Save them from loneliness and boredom;
    and watch over their families.

CARYL MICKLEM. *See note on p. 47.*

For those at sea

Eternal Father, strong to save,
Whose arm doth bind the restless wave,
Who bidd'st the mighty ocean deep
Its own appointed limits keep:
  O hear us when we cry to thee
  For those in peril on the sea.

O Saviour, whose almighty word
The winds and waves submissive heard,
Who walkedst on the foaming deep,
And calm amid its rage didst sleep:
  O hear us when we cry to thee
  For those in peril on the sea.

O sacred Spirit, who didst brood
Upon the chaos dark and rude,
Who bad'st its angry tumult cease,
And gavest light and life and peace:
  O hear us when we cry to thee
  For those in peril on the sea.

O Trinity of love and power,
Our brethren shield in danger's hour;
From rock and tempest, fire and foe,
Protect them whereso'er they go:
  And ever let there rise to thee
  Glad hymns of praise from land and sea.

WILLIAM WHITING *1825–78 for several years a master at Winchester College Choristers' School.*

For mariners

Helmsman	Be the ship blest.
Crew	By God the Father blest.
Helmsman	Be the ship blest.
Crew	And by God the Son blest.
Helmsman	Be the ship blest.
Crew	By God the Spirit blest.
All	God the Father,
	And God the Son,
	God the Spirit,
	Blessing give best,
	Be the ship blest.

Being of all,
The king of all,
Spirit of all,
Over our head eternal fall,
Near to us sure for evermore.

Traditional Gaelic prayer from ARCHIBALD
MACLLELLAN, *shipmaster in South Uist.*

For scientists

O Holy Wisdom of our God,
enlighten all men of science
who search out
the secrets of your creation,
that their humility before nature
may be matched by reverence towards you.
Save us from misusing their labours,
that the forces they set free
may enrich the life of man
and that your name may be hallowed
both in the search for truth
and in the use of power;
through Jesus Christ out Lord.

From the BBC's New Every Morning.

For neighbours

O Lord God,
I do from henceforth resolve,
    to love my neighbour as myself
    and to love him not in word only
    but in deed and in truth.
I do from my heart forgive all men their trespasses,
    do thou Lord forgive them also.
Lord bless those that hate me,
    and do good to them that have anyway
    despitefully used me,
    O repay them good for evil.
O my God, bless all those
    that I have anyway wronged.
Have mercy on all those to whose sins
    I have been anyway accessory
    and give them all grace to forgive me. Amen.

THOMAS KEN 1637–1711, *Bishop of Bath and Wells in
the late seventeenth century. Having taken an oath of
allegiance to James II before the king went into exile, he
refused to take the oath to William III. Deposed from his see,
he lived in retirement as one of the non-jurors. He wrote a
number of prayers and hymns.*

For neighbours

Lord God, you have taught us
   that we are members one of another
   and that none of us lives to himself alone:
we thank you for the community of which we are
   part;
   for those who share with us in its activities
   and for all who serve its varied interests.
Help us, as we have opportunity,
   to make our own contribution to the community
   and to learn to be good neighbours,
that by love we may serve one another;
   for the sake of Jesus Christ our Lord.

FRANK COLQUHOUN. *See note on p. 12.*

Lord Jesus, against whom no door can be shut,
enter the homes of our land,
and bless and guide us and our neighbours.
Grant that we may be so filled with your love
that we may truly love and serve one another,
showing courtesy, consideration and understanding.
Grant this, O Lord, for your dear Son's sake,
Jesus Christ our Saviour.

Mothers' Union Prayer Book.

For fellow-men

O God who have bound us together in this bundle
   of life,
      give us grace to understand how our lives depend
      upon the courage,
      the industry,
      the honesty,
      and the integrity of our fellow-men;
that we may be mindful of their needs,
      grateful for their faithfulness
      and constant in our responsibilities to them;
through Jesus Christ our Lord.

REINHOLD NIEBUHR *1892–1971, American theologian;
after being an evangelical pastor in working-class Detroit, he
became Professor of Christian Ethics at the Union
Theological Seminary, New York, from 1928 to 1960.*

For all who use the roads

Lord Jesus Christ,
who travelled the roads of Palestine
    to make known the gospel of the kingdom,
and who finally took the road
    that led to the Cross;
grant to us who use the roads
    such consideration for others
    as befits your servants,
and such a sense of your will and direction
    that we may journey always
    in faith and hope,
    for your great glory.

LLEWELLYN CUMINGS.

For members of a school community

We pray
For prefects and monitors
    and all to whom new authority and leadership is
        now to be entrusted,
    that they may act with courage, wisdom and
        fairness.

For new pupils, that they may give of their best in
        spirit, mind and body,
    and receive here only what is good.

For children who find the work difficult,
        that they may be helped to find new ways of
        developing their personalities
    and enriching their capacity for the service of
        others.

For games' teams, that they may play with
        enthusiasm, loyalty and unselfishness,
    and with a due sense of proportion.

For school societies, that they may flourish and
        prosper, to the good of all their members.

For the teaching staff, that their work may be
        carried out conscientiously
    and with the benefit of their pupils always in mind.

For the domestic staff, that they may have strength
        and cheerfulness for their duties
    and that no carelessness or ill manners on the part
        of others may make their lot difficult.

For those who conduct times of worship, that
        through them God will make his presence known
    and strengthen our wills for his service.

From A Book of Prayers for Schools.

For members of a school or college community

O God,
by whose providence
   the duties of mankind
   are variously ordered,
grant to all the members
   of this school
   such a spirit
   that we may labour heartily
   to do our work in our several stations.

Teach us to put to good account
   whatever talents
   you have lent us,
that as good and faithful servants
we may enter into the joy of our Lord.

BISHOP BROOKE FOSS WESTCOTT 1825–1901, *Regius Professor of Divinity at Cambridge from 1870 and later Bishop of Durham. The theological college, Westcott House, and the Cambridge Mission to Delhi owe much to his initiative.*

For the Queen

King of kings and Lord of lords,
  Remember all rulers
Whom thou has appointed to bear rule
  on the earth.
And among the first, be mindful of
  our gracious Queen,
And prosper her in all things;
And put into her heart good designs
  for thy church.
And for all thy people committed
  to her charge.
Grant unto her profound and undisturbed peace
  that in the tranquillity of her reign
we may lead a quiet and peaceful life,
  in all godliness and honesty.

LANCELOT ANDREWES. *See note on p. 55. His book of
private devotions, Preces Privatae was first published in 1648
and has been used throughout the following centuries. The
Queen referred to here is, of course, Elizabeth I.*

For the Queen

Pour your blessing, O God, we pray you,
upon Elizabeth our Queen, that she may fulfil her
    calling as a Christian ruler.
Support her in the ceaseless round of duty,
inspire her in the service of many peoples.
Give her wise and selfless ministers,
bless her in home and family
and grant that, through her, the Commonwealth
    may be knit together in one great brotherhood,
    a strength and joy to all its members
and an instrument of peace in our troubled world,
    through Jesus Christ, our Lord.

GEORGE APPLETON *b.*1902, *distinguished modern writer*
and compiler of prayers. He was Archbishop of Perth
1963–9 and Archbishop in Jerusalem 1969–74.

For the sovereign

To those who rule and lead us on the earth
you, sovereign Master,
have given their authority and kingship
– so marvellous that power of yours words fail to
    express –
that seeing the glory and honour
you have provided for them,
we should be subject to their rule,
not resisting your will.

Grant them, Lord,
the health, peace, control and stability
to use aright
the sovereignty you have bestowed on them.
For you, King of heaven, Lord of the ages, you it is
that give to mortal men
glory, honour and power
over what is on the earth.

Lord, make their counsels conform to what is good
and pleasing to you,
that using with reverence,
peacefully, gently,
the power you have given them,
they may find favour with you.

You alone have the means to do this for us,
this and more than this.
We thank you for it through Jesus Christ,
the High Priest, our souls' Protector.
Glory and splendour be yours through him,
now at this moment,
in every generation,
age after age. Amen.

CLEMENT OF ROME *end first century* AD, *one of the
earliest bishops of Rome. This prayer, written in the year* AD
96 *or thereabouts, is one of the earliest Christian prayers
outside scripture. It follows closely the Eighteen Blessings
recited daily by the Jews and provides an idea of improvised
prayer in early Christian times.*

For rulers

Almighty God,
from whom all thoughts of truth and peace proceed:
kindle, we pray, in the hearts of all men the true love
of peace;
and guide with your pure and peaceable wisdom
those who take counsel for the nations of the earth;
that in tranquillity your kingdom may go forward,
till the earth is filled with the knowledge of your
love;
through Jesus Christ our Lord.

Collect for Peace and Peacemakers. Alternative Service Book
1980.

For Queen and Parliament

Almighty God, by whom alone kings reign,
and princes decree justice;
and from whom alone cometh
all counsel, wisdom, and understanding;
We thine unworthy servants,
here gathered together in thy name,
do most humbly beseech thee
to send down thy heavenly wisdom from above,
to direct and guide us in all our consultations:
And grant that,
we having thy fear always before our eyes,
and laying aside all private interests,
prejudices, and partial affections,
the result of all our counsels may be
to the glory of thy blessed name,
the maintenance of true religion and justice,
the safety, honour, and happiness of the Queen,
the publick wealth, peace, and tranquillity of the
    realm,
and the uniting and knitting together of the hearts
of all persons and estates within the same,
in true Christian love and charity one towards
    another,
through Jesus Christ our Lord and Saviour. Amen.

*Prayers for Parliament used each day at the beginning of the
session by the Speaker's Chaplain.*

For Members of Parliament

Grant, O God, and continue to us
   a succession of legislators and rulers
   who have been taught the wisdom of the kingdom
      of Christ.
Endow all members of Parliament
   with a right understanding,
   a pure purpose and sound speech;
enable them to rise above all self-seeking and party
      zeal
   into the larger sentiments of public good
      and human brotherhood.
Purge our political life of every evil;
   subdue in the nation all unhallowed thirst for
      conquest or vainglory.
Inspire us with calmness and self-restraint,
   and the endeavour to have your will done
   everywhere upon the earth.

JOHN HUNTER 1849–1917, *minister of the Independent Chapel King's Weigh House in London.*

For leaders and peacemakers

Gracious Father,
we pray for peace in our world;
for all national leaders
that they may have wisdom to know
    and courage to do what is right;
for all men and women
    that their hearts may be turned to
    yourself in the search for
    righteousness and truth;
for those who are working to improve
    international relationships,
that they may find the true way of
    reconciliation;
for those who suffer as a result of war:
    the injured and disabled,
    the mentally distressed,
    the homeless and hungry,
    those who mourn for their dead,
    and especially for those
        who are without hope or friend
        to sustain them in their grief.

Baptist Peace Fellowship.

For peacemakers

Lord God,
we ask you to give courage and resolution
to those who are striving for peace and goodwill
in the industrial life of our country
and between nation and nation.
Grant that there may be greater tolerance and
   co-operation
   between management and labour
   and between people of different races.
Remove grievances and misunderstandings,
and let justice and equity prevail;
that all may strive together
in unity of purpose for the common good;
through Jesus Christ our Lord.

FRANK COLQUHOUN. *See note on p. 12.*

For members of local government

Guide, O Lord, we pray you,
   the mayor and councillors and workers in local
      government,
   with all, from the greatest to the least,
   who share in the ordering of our town:
And give strength, honour and charity to us
   and to all our fellow citizens:
that they may give their votes as in your sight and,
   seeking not their own,
   may see ever before them
   the vision of that free city, perfect in the heavens,
whose builder and maker is God.

PERCY DEARMER 1867–1936, *Vicar of St Mary's,
Primrose Hill, 1901–15; writer on ceremonial subjects and
religious music; he edited many books of hymns.*

For all ministers of healing

Bless, O Lord,
all who are co-operating in thy will for healing,
   all doctors, surgeons, nurses,
   psychiatrists, research workers,
   those who cook and clean,
   all who work in preventative health,
   all administrators,
   all who study our social life
   to help us how to live.
We thank you, O Lord of life and health,
   for this army of healing workers.
Praise be to you and gratitude to them.

GEORGE APPLETON. *See note on p. 74.*

For those who work for racial harmony

Lord,
strengthen the hands of those who work
 to draw together
 people of different races.
May the children who play together
 remain friendly
 as they grow older.
May students enter deeply
 into each other's worlds.
May those who live as neighbours
 or work together
 strive to create
 truly human bonds.

CARYL MICKLEM. *See note on p. 47.*

For the Jews

O God,
we are conscious that many centuries of blindness
  have blinded our eyes
so that we can no longer see the beauty
  of your chosen people,
nor recognise in their faces
  the features of our privileged brethren.
We realise that the mark of Cain
  stands upon our foreheads.
Across the centuries our brother Abel
  has lain in the blood which we drew
or which we caused to be shed by forgetting your
    love.
  Forgive us for the curse
we falsely attached to their name as Jews.
  Forgive us for crucifying you a second time
in their flesh. For we knew not what we did.

POPE JOHN XXIII 1881–1963, *called to the papacy at an*
advanced age, he nevertheless effected great changes in the
Roman Catholic Church by calling the Second Vatican
Council.

For those of other faiths

O God,
today and every day,
help me to see
all human beings
as my brothers and sisters,
made in your image,
and so may I always
live in and
by that light.

JOHN CARDEN b. 1924, former CMS missionary in
Pakistan who has also served in Bath, Amman and Geneva.

For the ministry

Lord God, bless all those whom you have called
to the ministry of the Church.
Deepen their understanding of faith,
so that they may share it with others.
Strengthen their commitment with love, hope and
    joy,
that their witness may be more effective.
Pour your grace upon them and their families,
and give them time for renewal of faith.
May they have the love and support of our prayers,
For Christ's sake.

MARGARET WILSON

Lord Jesus Christ, apostle, priest and servant,
bless the bishops, priests and deacons of your
    Church;
may they lead your people boldly,
walk with them lovingly,
and send them forth joyfully to proclaim
    the good news of
your kingdom, where you live for ever and ever.

Advisory Board of Ministry (ABM).

For fellow Christians

O Father,
give perfection to beginners,
intelligence to the young ones,
aid to those who are running their course.
Give sorrow to the negligent,
zeal of spirit to the lukewarm,
and to those who have attained, a good ending,
for the sake of Christ Jesus, our Lord.

ST IRENAEUS c. AD 130–c.200, *theologian, Bishop of Lyons.*

For Christians

Grant, we beseech thee, merciful Lord,
  to thy faithful people
    pardon and peace;
that they may be cleansed from all their sins,
  and serve thee
    with a quiet mind;
through Jesus Christ our Lord. Amen.

THOMAS CRANMER 1489–1556, *Archbishop of
Canterbury from 1532 until he was burnt at the stake in
1556; he was largely responsible for translating into English
the Collects, from ancient texts, of the First Prayer Book of
Edward VI of 1549.*

For Christians

Grant more of your Spirit to all your churches and
    servants in the world;
that as their darkness and selfishness and
    imperfections
have defiled and divided and weakened them,
and made them scandalous and harsh towards
    unbelievers,
so may their knowledge, self-denial and impartial
    love
truly reform, unite and strengthen them:
that the glory of their holiness
may win an unbelieving world to
        Christ.

RICHARD BAXTER *1615–91, Puritan divine; he was a
prolific writer and champion of moderation.*

For members of the Church

Lord God, our heavenly Father,
grant to your Church today
    the faith of her apostles
    the hope of her martyrs
    and the love of her Lord,
even Jesus Christ, in whose name we pray.

CHRISTOPHER IDLE. *See note on p. 62.*

Lord God, we thank you
For calling us into the company of those
Who trust in Christ and seek to do his will.
May your Spirit guide and strengthen us
In mission and service to your world;
For we are strangers no longer
But pilgrims together on the way to your kingdom.

Prayer of the Inter-Church Process made at Swanwick in 1989.

PRAYERS
FOR THOSE WHO
ARE SUFFERING

For the hungry

I saw a child today, Lord,
who will not die tonight,
harried into a hunger's grave.
He was bright and full of life,
because his father has a job
and feeds him.
But somewhere, everywhere,
ten thousand life-lamps
will go out,
and not be lit tomorrow.
Lord, teach me my sin.

Prayer of an African Christian, Anglican Cycle of Prayer.

For the hungry

Lord of the harvest,
we rejoice in the bounty of your world;
we thank you for the rich harvest it produces.
We remember those who do not have enough,
the thousands who are dying of hunger each day.
We pray for those who have more than they require.
We pray for ourselves and our churches:
show us what needs to be done,
and how to share the world's harvest more fairly.
Teach us to value people more than things.
Above all, help us to set our hearts
on your kingdom of love and justice,
and to seek to do your will here on earth,
as servants of Jesus Christ our Lord.

Christian Aid

For the poor and hungry

Make us worthy, Lord,
To serve our fellow-men
Throughout the world who live and die
In poverty and hunger.
Give them, through our hands
this day their daily bread,
and by our understanding love,
Give peace and joy.

MOTHER TERESA OF CALCUTTA *b. 1910, of Albanian
origin. In 1950 she founded the Missionaries of Charity
Sisters for the relief of suffering in the slums of Calcutta.*

For those in need

Almighty Father
whose Son Jesus Christ has taught us
that what we do for the least of our brethren
   we do also for him;
give us the will to be the servant of others
   as he was the servant of all,
who gave up his life and died for us,
but is alive and reigns with you and the Holy Spirit,
one God, now and for ever.

Alternative Service Book 1980, *Collect for the 11th Sunday in Pentecost.*

Help us
Cease to do evil.
Learn to do good,
Search for justice,
help the oppressed, the poor, the starving, the
   elderly,
   the lonely, the imprisoned,
be just to the orphan, the unmarried mother, the
   mentally and physically disabled,
plead for the widow, the refugee and the immigrant.
Let us go in peace and serve the Lord,
In the name of Christ, Amen.

SHEILA CASSIDY *b. 1937, Roman Catholic doctor and writer who went to work in Chile in 1971, where she suffered imprisonment and torture as a result of treating a wounded guerrilla.*

For those in need

O Lord, we know that we live in a world of plenty,
  with food sufficient for all.
Help us to realise that there is enough
  for everyone's need.
But not enough for everyone's greed.
  Give us hearts of compassion,
  unselfish concern and loving care,
that all may have the abundant life
  which is your will.
When we offer all that we have,
  we know that in your hands
  there is enough and to spare.
O Lord of the hungry crowd
  and of the twelve basketsful left over.

GEORGE APPLETON. *See note on p. 74.*

For the sick

O God the Creator and Father of all men,
We praise you that your will is life
   and health and strength.
Help all who are ill or in pain
   to place themselves in your hands
     in loving trust,
so that your healing life may flow into them
   to make them well and strong,
   able and ready to do your holy will;
through him who has made known to us
   both your love and your will,
even Jesus Christ our Lord.

GEORGE APPLETON. *See note on p. 74.*

For patients in hospital

Lord God, whose son, Jesus Christ, understood
people's fear and pain before they spoke of them,
we pray for those in hospital;
surround the frightened with your tenderness;
give strength to those in pain;
hold the weak in your arms of love,
and give hope and patience to those who are
      recovering;
we ask this through the same Jesus Christ, our Lord.

CHRISTINE MCMULLEN

For the seemingly incurable

O heavenly Father,
we pray for those suffering from diseases
for which there is at present no cure.
Give them the victory of trust and hope,
that they may never lose their faith
in your loving purpose.
Grant your wisdom to all
who are working to discover the causes of disease,
and the realisation that through you
all things are possible.
We ask this in the name of him
who went about doing good
and healing all manner of sickness,
even your Son, Jesus Christ, our Lord.

GEORGE APPLETON. *See note on p. 74.*

For the departed

Unto him who is gone hence, O my Saviour,
　　open thou, we beseech thee,
the door of thy mercy, O Christ;
that he may rejoice in glory,
　　as he partakes of the joys of your kingdom.

What pleasure in this life remains unmarked by
　　　sorrow?
What glory can endure upon this earth
　　　unchanged?
All is feebler than a shadow,
　　more deceptive than a dream;
for death in a single moment takes all things away.
But in the light of thy countenance, O Christ,
　　and in the joy of thy beauty,
　　give rest to those whom thou hast chosen,
for thou lovest mankind.

Orthodox Prayer for the Dead.

For the dead

May he be with God.
May he be with the living God.
May he be with the immortal God.
May he be in God's hands.
May he be where the great name of God is.
May he be where God's greatness is.
May he be with the living God
now and on the day of judgment.
Live in God, live in eternal delight.

Acclamations were an early form of prayer. Some were cut in stone upon tombs, such as this example from earliest Christian times.

For the blind

O God, the source of all light,
lighten the darkness of those
who have no sight,
illuminate their inward vision,
and let them rest in thee;
for the sake of Jesus Christ our Lord.

Guild of St Raphael, founded in 1915 to work for the restoration of the Ministry of Healing as part of the normal function of the Church. Their activities include teaching and preparing the sick, as well as intercession.

For victims of cruelty

We pray for the world's problems and needs . . .
We pray for the sick heart of man —
    still, as it has always been,
    capable of great heights,
    but also of hideous depths.
We pray for the victims of anger
    and of calculated cruelty and brutality,
    and for all passing through
    any kind of affliction.
Use human sympathy and kindness
    to bring home the reality of divine power
    and compassion,
so that the gracious Lord may be known
    through the gracious neighbour.
These prayers, and all the unspoken longings
    of our hearts,
    we bring before you
    in the confidence of those
    who heard their Master say
'The man who comes to me I will never turn away'.

CARYL MICKLEM. *See note on p. 47.*

For the grievously afflicted

Lord, the wounds of the world
are too deep for us to heal.
We have to bring men and women to you
and ask you to look after them –
the sick in body and mind,
the withered in spirit,
the victims of greed and injustice,
the prisoners of grief.
And yet, our Father,
do not let our prayers excuse us
from paying the price of compassion.
Make us generous with the resources
you have entrusted to us.
Let your work of rescue be done
in us and through us all.

CARYL MICKLEM. *See note on p.* 47.

For the sick in mind

O Holy Spirit who searches out all things,
even the deep things of God
and the deep things of man,
we pray you to penetrate into the springs
    of personality
of those who are sick in mind,
to bring them cleansing,
        healing
        and unity.
Sanctify all memory,
        dispel all fear,
and bring them to love you
        with all their mind and will,
that they may be made whole and glorify
        you for ever.
We ask this in the name of him
        who cast out devils
        and healed men's minds,
even Jesus Christ our Lord.

GEORGE APPLETON. *See note on p. 74.*

For those who have taken their own lives

Almighty God, Father of all mankind,
have mercy on all those
  who in their darkness
  have thrown away their mortal lives.
Grant them light and salvation,
  that they may find new life in your love
and glorify your holy name.

AUDREY MARSHALL

For the homeless

Have mercy, O Lord,
on those whom war
or oppression
or famine
have robbed of homes
and friends,
and prosper all
who help them.
We commend also
to your care
those whose homes
are broken
by conflict
and lack of love.
Grant that where
our love has failed,
the divine compassion
may heal.

Anglican Cycle of Prayer.

For refugees

We pray, Lord,
for all those who have been forced
    to leave home and country.
We pray that as many as possible
    may find a new home,
    work that satisfies them
    and a country they can love.
And for those who remain in refugee camps,
    we pray that there may yet be hope
    of a new and worthwhile life.

CARYL MICKLEM. *See note on p. 47.*

For those who provoke war and aggression

O Lord Jesus Christ,
who in the hour of your agony
prayed for those who nailed you to the Cross;
enable us, by the might of the Holy Spirit,
to pray for aggressors.
Break the power of all
who seek domination and delight in war;
open the eyes of all who are blinded
    by fear, idolatry or hate;
strengthen the hands of all who love
    truth and right, that
when this dread necessity of strife be passed,
    we may with them seek justice in the earth
and freedom in the souls of men.

From the BBC's New Every Morning.

For prisoners

We pray, our Father, for those
whose freedom has been taken from them;
for all who suffer imprisonment,
whether for crime or conscience sake;
for all whose vision of your world
is seen through bars,
and in whose heart the lamp of hope burns low.
God of mercy, give them help,
according to their need,
and hear our prayer
for Jesus Christ's sake.

TIMOTHY DUDLEY-SMITH *b. 1926, Suffragan Bishop of Thetford 1981–92 and President of the Evangelical Alliance 1987–1991. He is a popular hymnwriter.*

For the unemployed

Lord Christ, you said to your disciples,
'My Father has worked till now, and I work':
we pray for those who through no fault of their own
have been deprived of the work
that leads towards the fulfilment of their lives.
Inspire and guide those
who bear the responsibility of finding the answer
to our industrial problems.
Open their minds to the truth,
that they may discern in the events of our time
the direction of your will;
and give them the courage to declare
what they believe to be right,
and the power to carry it through.

BASIL NAYLOR. *See note on p. 62.*

For the bereaved

We remember, Lord, the slenderness
of the thread which separates life from death,
and the suddenness with which it can be broken.
Help us also to remember that
on both sides of that division
we are surrounded by your love.
Persuade our hearts that when our dear ones die,
neither we nor they are parted from you.
In you may we find peace,
and in you be united with them
in the glorious body of Christ,
who has burst the bonds of death,
and is alive for evermore,
our Saviour and theirs
for ever and ever. Amen.

DICK WILLIAMS

PRAYERS
FOR OURSELVES

For ourselves

Our Father in heaven,
hallowed be your name,
your kingdom come,
your will be done,
on earth as in heaven.
Give us today our daily bread.
Forgive us our sins
as we forgive those who sin against us.
Lead us not into temptation
but deliver us from evil.

For the kingdom, the power and the glory
   are yours
now and for ever. Amen.

For ourselves

Blessed you are, Lord;
show me what you want me to do.
Lord, you have been our refuge
from generation to generation.
Lord, have mercy on me
– I ask as I have asked before –
heal this soul that has sinned against you.
Teach me to do your will,
for you are my God.
In you is the source of all life;
in you is the light
whereby we shall see light.
Forever show your mercy
to them that have come to know you.

From an early fragment of the Te Deum, *translated by A. Hamman* OP.

For ourselves

O Lord God,
who has given me the gift of sight,
grant that I may see
   not only with the eyes of my head,
   but with the eyes of the heart also,
that I may perceive the beauty
   and meaning of all that I behold,
and glorify you,
   the Creator of all,
   who are blessed for evermore.

GEORGE APPLETON. *See note on p. 74.*

For ourselves

Be silent
still
aware
for there
in your own heart
the Spirit is at prayer
listen and learn
open and find
heart-wisdom
Christ.

Prayer from Malling Abbey, a House of Anglican Benedictine Nuns.

All we need, good Lord, is you yourself;
not words about you, but your very presence.
   In the silence.
   In the stillness.
Come, Lord, Come.

RICHARD HARRIES *b. 1936, Dean of King's College, London 1981–7. Bishop of Oxford from 1987 and well-known as an author and broadcaster.*

For ourselves

Lord,
may I ever speak
as though it were the last word
that I can speak.
May I ever act
as though it were the last action
that I can perform.
May I ever suffer
as though it were the last pain
that I can offer.
May I ever pray
as though it were for me on earth
the last chance
to speak to you.

CHIARA LUBICH b. 1920, *Italian founder of the Focolare
Movement for living by the Gospel in the world.*

For ourselves – in old age

Almighty Father, Son and Holy Spirit,
eternal, blessed and gracious God,
allow me, the least of saints,
   to keep open a door in paradise,
the smallest and least-used door, the furthest door,
only so long as it is in your house, O God,
and I can see your glory from afar,
and hear your voice,
and know that I am with you, my God.

ST COLUMBA, AD 521–97, *Abbot and missionary in Ireland and Scotland.*

For ourselves

We pray that God, the Father,
and the eternal High Priest, Jesus Christ,
may nurture us
in faith, truth and love,
and grant us our portion among the saints,
and all who believe in our Lord Jesus Christ.
We pray for all the people of Christ,
for rulers and leaders,
for all the enemies of his cross,
and for ourselves
that our fruit may increase,
and we be made perfect
in Christ Jesus our Lord.

ST POLYCARP c. AD 69–155, *Bishop of Smyrna, martyred
by the sword and by fire at the age of 86.*

For ourselves

Dear Father in heaven
let us be peacemakers
more ready to call people friends than enemies
more ready to trust than to mistrust
more ready to love than to hate
more ready to respect than despise
more ready to serve than be served
more ready to absorb evil than to pass it on.
Dear Father in heaven,
let us be more like Christ.

The Mothers' Union

Lord God, whose we are and whom we serve:
    we place our lives afresh in your hands.
Take us as we are;
    and make us what you would have us be;
and so fill us with your Holy Spirit
    that we may be strong for your service
    and used wholly for your glory;
through Jesus Christ our Lord.

FRANK COLQUHOUN. *See note on p. 12.*

For ourselves

Almighty God,
you have provided the resources of the world
to maintain the life of your children,
and have so ordered our life
that we are dependent upon each other.
Bless all men in their daily work,
and as you have given us the knowledge to produce
    plenty,
so give us the will to bring it within the reach of all;
through Jesus Christ our Lord.

Collect for Rogation days (intercession for the harvest).
Alternative Service Book 1980.

For ourselves

Give me, O Lord, a steadfast heart,
   which no unworthy thought can drag downwards,
an unconquered heart,
   which no tribulation can wear out;
an upright heart,
   which no unworthy purpose may tempt aside.
Bestow upon me also, O Lord my God,
   understanding to know thee,
   diligence to seek thee,
   wisdom to find thee,
and a faithfulness that may finally embrace thee;
   through Jesus Christ our Lord.

THOMAS AQUINAS c. *1225–74, Dominican theologian
and philosopher; author of the celebrated* 'Summa
Theologica'.

For ourselves

Lord Jesus Christ,
fill us, we pray, with your light and love,
that we may reflect your wondrous glory.
So fill us with your love
that we may count nothing too small to do for you,
nothing too much to give,
and nothing too hard to bear.

IGNATIUS LOYOLA 1491–1556, a Spaniard who founded the Jesuit Order in 1534 and wrote the Spiritual Exercises which are still widely used today.

For ourselves – for spiritual comfort

Father in heaven,
As on other occasions
   the intercession of the congregation
   is that you would comfort
   all them that are sick and sorrowful,
so now at this hour
   its intercession is that to them
   that labour and are heavy laden
   you would give rest for their souls.
Oh, and yet this is hardly an intercession.
   Who might count himself so sound
   that he need only pray for others?
Ah, no, everyone prays on his own account
   that you would give him rest for his soul.
O God, to each one severally
   whom you behold labouring and heavy laden
   with the consciousness of sin,
   give rest to his soul.

SÖREN KIERKEGAARD *1813–55, a Danish philosopher
whose later religious books had considerable influence on
contemporary thought.*

For ourselves

Grant unto us O Lord,
   the royalty of inward happiness
   and the serenity which comes from living close to
      thee.
Daily renew in us the sense of joy
   and let thy eternal spirit
   dwell in our souls and bodies,
   filling every corner of our hearts with light and
      gladness;
so that, bearing about with us
   the infection of a good courage,
   we may be diffusers of life,
and meet all that comes, of good or ill,
   even death itself,
   with gallant and high hearted happiness:
giving thee thanks always for all things. Amen.

*Prayer for the Annual Service of the Distinguished Order of
St Michael and St George for service to the Crown.*

For ourselves

O God we are one with you.
You have made us one with you.
You have taught us that if we are open to one
    another,
  you dwell in us.
Help us to preserve this openness and to fight for it
    with all our hearts.
Help us to realise that there can be no understanding
  where there is mutual rejection.
O God, in accepting one another wholeheartedly,
    fully, completely,
we accept you, and we thank you, and we adore
    you;
and we love you with our whole being,
  because our being is in your being,
    our spirit is rooted in your spirit.
Fill us then with love,
and let us be bound together with love as we go our
    diverse ways,
united in this one spirit which makes you present to
    the world,
and which makes you witness to the ultimate reality
  that is love.
Love has overcome.
Love is victorious.
Amen.

THOMAS MERTON 1915–68, *an American Cistercian
monk who became a prolific spiritual writer. During the
latter part of his life he developed an interest in Eastern
religions.*

For ourselves

Fix thou our steps, O Lord, that we stagger not at the uneven motions of the world, but steadily go on to our glorious home; neither censuring our journey by the weather we meet with, nor turning out of the way for anything that befalls us. The winds are often rough, and our own weight presses us downwards.

Reach forth, O Lord, thy hand, thy saving hand, and speedily deliver us.

JOHN WESLEY *1703—91, preacher and evangelist, he was one of the founders of the Methodist movement, though he remained a member of the Church of England throughout his life.*

For ourselves

Lord Jesus,
I give you my hands to do your work,
I give you my feet to go your way.
I give you my eyes to see as you do.
I give you my tongue to speak your words.
I give you my mind that you may think in me.
I give you my spirit that you may pray in me.
Above all,
I give you my heart that you may love in me,
    your Father, and all mankind.
I give you my whole self that you may grow in me,
    so that it is you, Lord Jesus,
who live and work and pray in me.

LANCELOT ANDREWES. *See note on p. 55.*

For ourselves – in bereavement

O Lord our God,
from whom neither life nor death
   can separate us
   from those who trust in your love,
and whose love holds in its embrace
   your children in this world
   and in the next,
so unite us to yourself,
   that in fellowship with you
   we may be always united
   to our loved ones
   whether here or there:
give us courage, constancy and hope;
through him who died and was buried
   and rose again for us,
   Jesus Christ our Lord.

WILLIAM TEMPLE. *See note on p. 42. He wrote this prayer for his wife at the time of the death of her mother.*

For ourselves

Into thy hands,
O Lord and Father,
We commend our souls and our bodies,
Our parents and our homes,
Friends, neighbours and kindred,
Our benefactors and brethren departed,
All thy people faithfully believing,
And all who need thy pity and protection.
Enlighten us with thy holy grace,
And suffer us never more
To be separated from thee,
Who art one God in Trinity,
God everlasting.

ST EDMUND RICH *1170–1240, also known as Edmund of Abingdon, he became Archbishop of Canterbury in 1233 and was canonised in 1247.*

Acknowledgements

The compiler and publishers are pleased to acknowledge the following for permission to quote from their copyright material:

G. Appleton, for 'O Holy Spirit who searches out all things' from *Daily Prayer and Praise*, World Christian Books (Lutterworth, 1966).

G. Appleton, for 'O God who have bound us together in this bundle of life', 'Bless, O Lord, all who are co-operating', 'O heavenly Father, we pray for those suffering from diseases', 'O Lord, we know that we live in a world of plenty', and 'Give me, O Lord, a steadfast heart' from *Journey for a Soul* (Fontana, Collins, 1974).

G. Appleton (ed.), for 'Lord, keep my parents in your love', 'Almighty God, have mercy on all that bear me evil will', 'Unto him who is gone hence, O my Saviour', 'Make us worthy, Lord, to serve our fellow-men', 'Pour your blessing, O God, we pray you', and 'O Lord God, who has given me the gift of sight' from *Oxford Book of Prayer* (Oxford University Press, 1988).

N. Autton, for 'O God the Creator and Father of all men' and 'O God, the source of all light' from *A Manual of Prayers and Readings with the Sick* (SPCK, 1970).

A. E. Baker, for 'O Lord our God, from whom neither life nor death can separate us' from *William Temple and his Message* (Penguin).

W. Barclay, for 'Thank you, if the passing of the years has made me understand my parents better', 'O God, help me to be true to the great privilege and the great responsibility which you have given to me', and 'O God, help me always to remember that you have given to me the most important task in the world' from *More Prayers for the Plain Man* (Fontana, Collins, 1962).

W. Barclay, for 'O God, our Father, we give you thanks', 'O God our Father, as our child goes to school for the first time', and 'O God, our Father, whose greatest gift is love' from *The Plain Man's Book of Prayers* (Fount, Collins, 1977).

BBC, for 'O heavenly Father, who has bestowed on us', 'O Holy Wisdom of our God', 'O Lord Jesus Christ, who in the hour of your agony', and 'We pray, our Father, for those whose freedom has been taken from them' from *New Every Morning, A Book of Daily Prayers for Broadcasting* (BBC, rev. 1948).

E. Blyton, for 'In the morning, thank you, Lord Jesus' from *Before I go the Sleep: A Book of Stories and Prayers for Children* (Latimer House, 1947).

J. Carden, for 'O God, today and every day' from *Another Day* (Triangle, SPCK, 1986).

Sheila Cassidy, for 'Help us cease to do evil' from *Prayer for Pilgrims* (Fount/Harper, Collins 1980).

T. Castle (ed.), for 'Lord Jesus Christ, I praise and thank you for my parents', 'Heavenly Father, from whom all parenthood comes', 'Lord, teach me to love my grandchildren', and 'Into thy hands, O Lord and Father' from *The Family Book of Prayers* (McCrimmons, 1988).

F. Colquhoun (ed.), for 'Lord God, you have taught us', 'Eternal God, author of harmony and happiness', 'Lord Jesus Christ, who travelled the roads of Palestine', 'Father, we thank you that you have spoken to us through the words of scripture', 'Lord God, our heavenly Father, grant to your church today', 'Almighty God, Father of all Mankind' from *Contemporary Parish Prayers* (Hodder & Stoughton, 1975).

F. Colquhoun (ed.), for 'God of Love, we pray for our children', and 'Lord Jesus, thank you for being our friend' from *Family Prayers* (Triangle, SPCK, 1984).

F. Colquhoun (ed.), for 'Eternal Father, strong to save', 'Heavenly Father, you are present everywhere', 'Lord God, whose we are and whom we serve', 'Lord God, you have placed in human hands', and 'Lord Christ, you said to your disciples', from *New Parish Prayers* (Hodder & Stoughton, 1982).

F. Colquhoun, (ed.), for 'Lord God, we ask you to give courage', 'Most gracious Father, this is our home', 'Heavenly Father, marriage is of your making', 'May the God of love who is the source of all our affection', and 'Our Father, we remember before you' from *Prayers for Today* (Triangle, SPCK, 1989).

P. D. deFevre, for 'Father in Heaven, as on other occasions' from *The Prayers of Kierkegaard* (University of Chicago Press).

Canon Donald Gray, for 'Almighty God, by whom alone kings reign'.

A. Hamman (ed.), for 'To those who rule and lead us on the earth', 'May he be with God', and 'Blessed you are, Lord' from *Early Christian Prayers* (Longmans Green, 1961).

R. Harries, for 'All we need, good Lord, is you yourself' from *Prayer and the Pursuit of Happiness* (Fount, Collins, 1985).

C. Hunt (ed.), for 'Richard, run ryghte' and 'O Lord, give me strength to refrain' from *Uncommon Prayers* (Hodder & Stoughton, 1963).

H. Martin (ed.), for 'We pray for prefects and monitors', 'O God, by whose providence', 'Grant, O God, and continue to us' and 'Guide O Lord, we pray you' from *A Book of Prayers for Schools* (SCM, 1936).

C. Micklem (ed.), for 'Let us pray for our friends', 'We remember with gratitude, Father', 'We pray for those who go to sea', 'Lord, strengthen the hands of those who work', 'We pray for the world's problems and needs', and 'We pray, Lord, for all those who have been forced to leave home and country' from *Contemporary Prayers for Church and School* (SCM).

C. Micklem (ed.), for 'Lord, the wounds of the world are too deep for us to heal' from *Contemporary Prayers for Public Worship* (SCM).

Mothers' Union, for 'O God, our heavenly Father, we pray for your grace', 'O God, our Father, we ask you to bless those who have entered our family life', 'Lord God, bless all those whom you have called', 'Lord God, whose son, Jesus Christ, understood people's fear and pain', and 'Dear Father in heaven, let us be peacemakers' from Anthology of *Public Prayers* (Mothers' Union).

Mothers' Union, for 'Lord Jesus, against whom no door can be shut' from *Mothers' Union Prayer Book*.

Mothers' Union, 'Holy God, Creator and Father', 'We thank you, God our Father', and 'Heavenly Father, look in love on all our friends and neighbours' from *Prayers and Praise* (Mothers' Union).

D. M. Owen (ed.), for 'O Father, give perfection to beginners', 'Almighty Father, Son and Holy Spirit', 'We pray that God, the Father, and the eternal High Priest, Jesus Christ', 'Fix thou our steps, O Lord' and 'Lord Jesus, I give you my hands to do your work' from *Something of a Saint* (Triangle, SPCK, 1990).

Penguin Books, for 'Jesus Christ, my dear and gracious Lord' and 'Almighty and tender Lord Jesus Christ' from *The Prayers and Meditations of St Anselm*, tr. from Latin by Sister Benedicta Ward (Penguin, 1973).

M. Reith, for 'I send my heart to thee in thanks for these little ones', 'Yours be the blessing of God and the Lord', 'Be the ship blest', 'Thou seest me, Father, stand before my cottage', and 'May God, my dear, be thy healing one' from *God in Our Midst* (Triangle, SPCK, 1989).

R. Runcie and B. Hume (eds), for 'Gracious Father, we pray for peace in our world' from *Prayers for Peace* (SPCK, 1987).

M. H. Shepherd Jnr (ed.), for 'O God of love and mercy' from *A Companion of Prayer for Daily Living* (Morehouse–Barlow, USA).

R. S. Thomas, for 'I look up, you pass' from *Later Poems: A Selection* (Macmillan, 1983).

D. Williams, for 'We remember, Lord, the slenderness of the thread' from *More Prayers for Today's Church* (Kingsway/CPAS).

Quotations from *The Alternative Service Book 1980* are copyright © The Central Board of Finance of the Church of England.

Every effort has been made to trace the copyright holders of material quoted in this book. Information on any omissions should be sent to the publishers who will make full acknowledgement in future editions.